REDBACK
publishing

First Published 2026 by
Redback Publishing
Suite 6, 13a Narabang Way,
Belrose NSW 2085
Australia

www.redbackpublishing.com
orders@redbackpublishing.com

ISBN 978-1-761402-03-6

Author: John Lesley
Editor: Lucinda Dodds and Emma Dobinson
Designer: Redback Publishing

Original illustrations © Redback Publishing 2026
Originated by Redback Publishing

Acknowledgements
Abbreviations: l—left, r—right, b—bottom, t—top, c—centre, m—middle
We would like to thank the following for permission to reproduce photographs (images © Shutterstock unless otherwise stated) p24bl & p25tl antony trivet photography / Shutterstock.com

A catalogue record for this book is available from the National Library of Australia

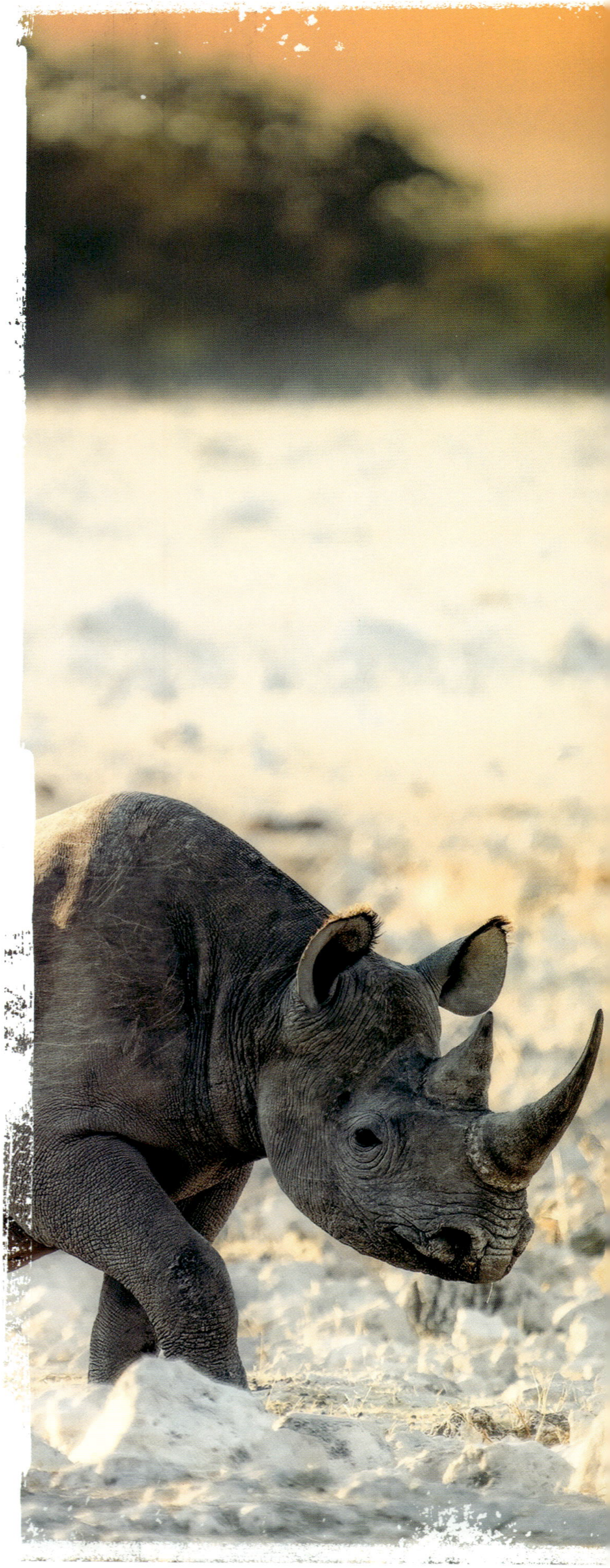

CONTENTS

WHAT IS A RHINO?

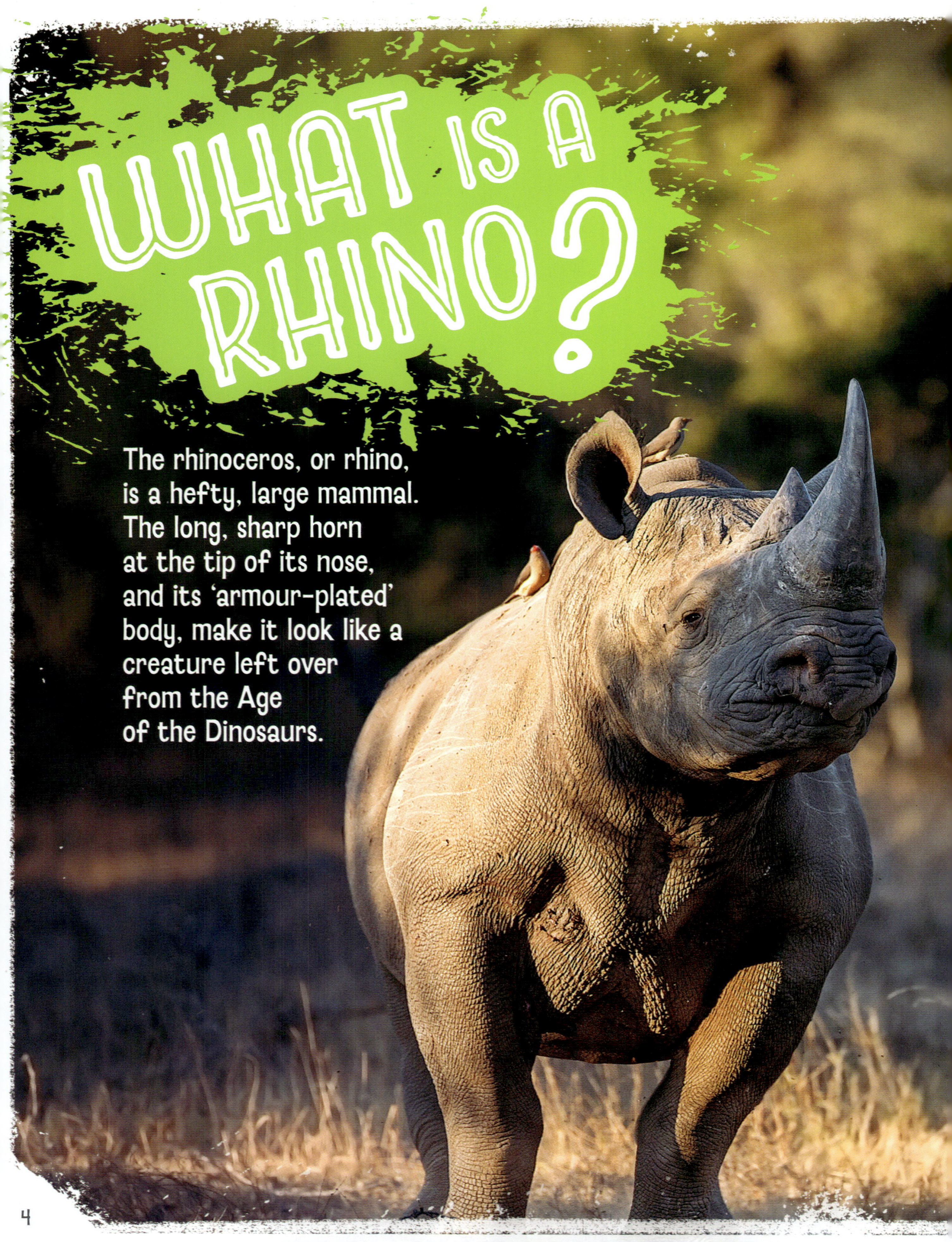

The rhinoceros, or rhino, is a hefty, large mammal. The long, sharp horn at the tip of its nose, and its 'armour-plated' body, make it look like a creature left over from the Age of the Dinosaurs.

Despite its appearance, the rhino is not related to the extinct dinosaurs, but it is amongst the few megafauna that still exist. Megafauna are oversized animals that mostly became extinct thousands of years ago. The rhino, hippo, elephant and giraffe are a few of the megafauna that have managed to survive until the present.

UNICORN OR RHINO?

The rhino may be the original unicorn. Travellers in the distant past saw rhinos and took home stories of a four-legged animal with a long horn. Over time, the hefty rhino in those stories changed into an elegant unicorn.

RHINO BASIC FACTS

HORNS

The horns are made of keratin, which is the same substance that forms human hair and fingernails.

The name rhinoceros comes from an ancient Greek word that refers to a horn on the nose.

THERE ARE FIVE SPECIES OF RHINO ALIVE TODAY:

White rhinoceros *Ceratotherium simum*
Black rhinoceros *Diceros bicornis*
Sumatran rhinoceros *Dicerorhinus sumatrensis*
Javan rhinoceros *Rhinoceros sondaicus*
Greater one-horned rhinoceros *Rhinoceros unicornis*

DUNG HEAPS

Rhinos often leave their droppings together in large dung heaps that can be metres wide. The heaps are made in places where rhinos communicate with each other through smell.

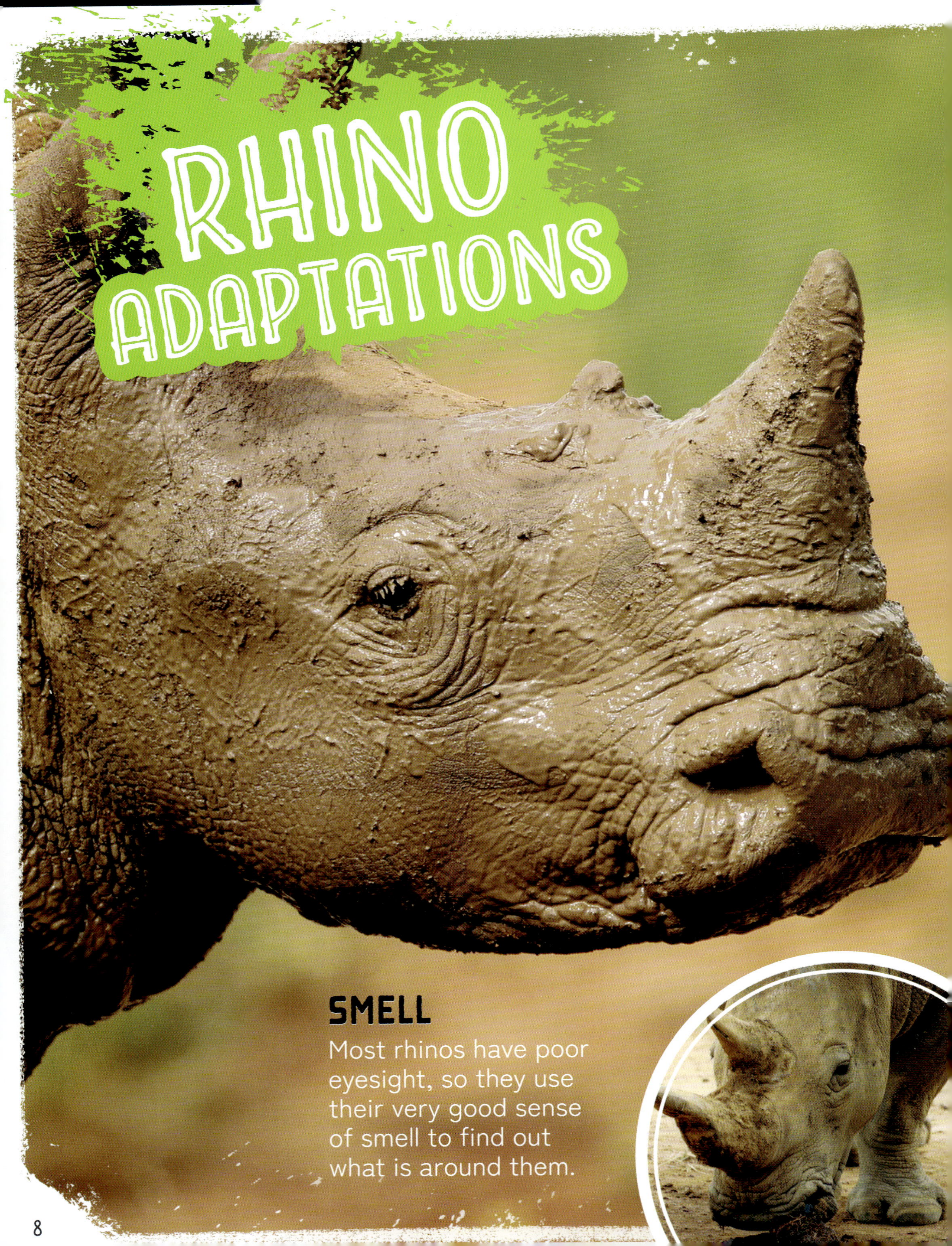

RHINO ADAPTATIONS

SMELL

Most rhinos have poor eyesight, so they use their very good sense of smell to find out what is around them.

LIPS

Some rhino species use their lips like fingers to choose the best parts of a plant to eat.

ARMOUR

Rhino skin can be over four centimetres thick on some parts of the body. The skin is usually hairless, or may be sparsely haired, and is covered in bumps. It acts like armour for the rhino, protecting it against predators. Lions, hyenas and tigers occasionally kill a small or sick rhino, but they are less successful trying to kill a healthy adult.

Despite its thickness, the skin needs constant attention by the rhino to stop it burning. They wallow in mud to cover themselves, and this gives them protection from sunburn and from insects.

SMART?

They have a reputation for not being very smart, and they do indeed have small brains for their size. However, never underestimate a rhino. They have survived on Earth for millions of years, so they must be doing something right.

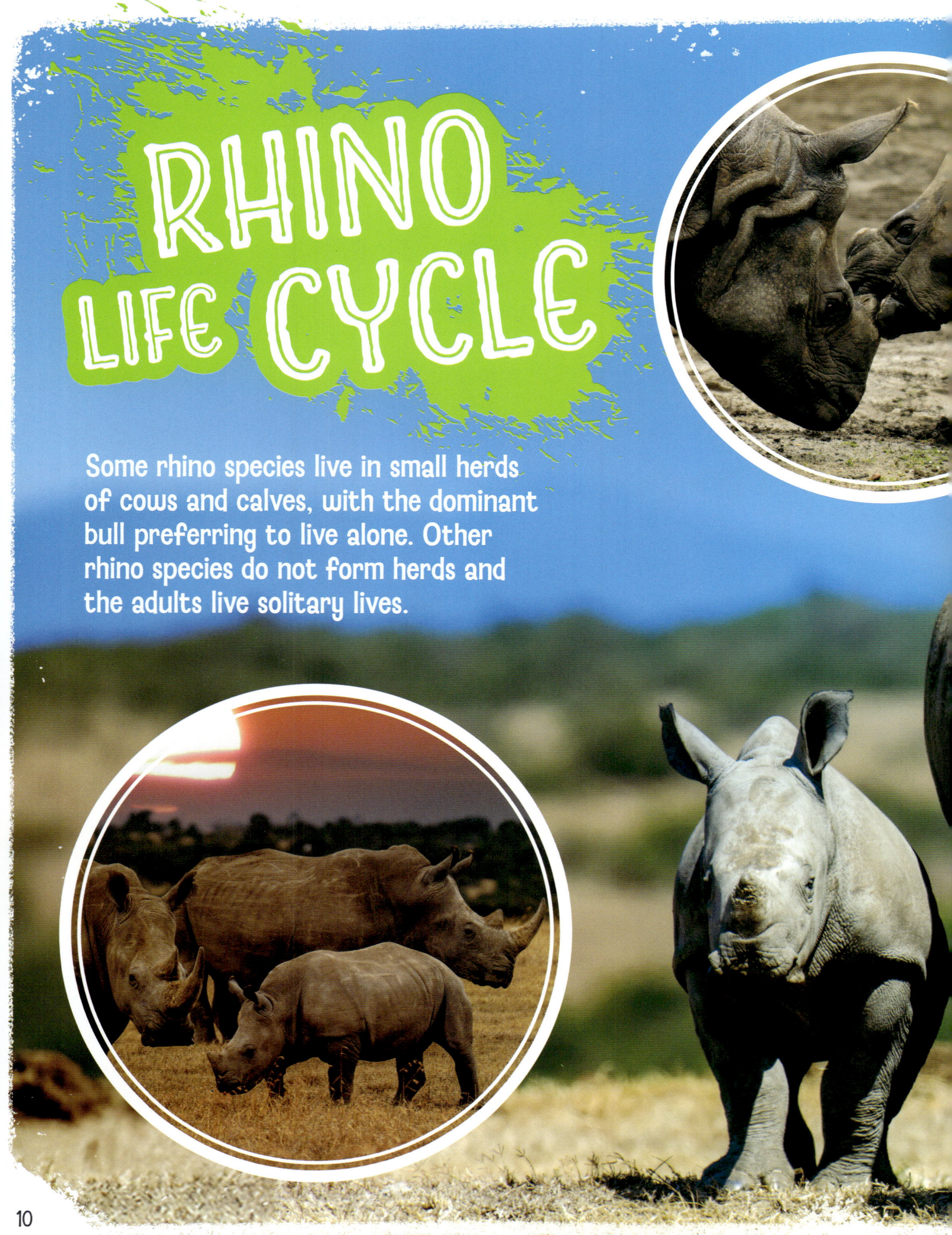

RHINO LIFE CYCLE

Some rhino species live in small herds of cows and calves, with the dominant bull preferring to live alone. Other rhino species do not form herds and the adults live solitary lives.

Rhinos have a very long pregnancy of about 15-16 months, giving birth to just one calf. Calves weigh about 50 kilograms, depending on the species of rhino. They stay with their mother for about two years and sometimes much longer.

Rhinos are slow breeders, which is one of the reasons their continued existence is under threat.

Rhinos live for 30-50 years in the wild.

FIVE TYPES OF RHINO

1 WHITE RHINO

SCIENTIFIC NAME:
Ceratotherium simum

OTHER NAME:
Square-lipped rhinoceros

COLOUR: Grey skin

HORN: Two horns, the larger one growing to over half a metre long

COMMON SIZE: 4 metres in length, 2 tonnes in weight

HABITAT: Savannah grasslands of central and southern Africa

FOOD: Grazes on grass

The white rhino is not actually white.

THERE ARE TWO TYPES OF WHITE RHINO:

Southern white rhino:
Fewer than 20,000 in the wild

Northern white rhino:
Close to extinction in 2026. Only two females are known to exist.

SUDAN
THE LAST MALE NORTHERN
WHITE RHINO
1973 - 2018

The last male northern white rhino died in 2018.

BODY

The white rhino is one of the largest land animals in the world, and the largest of all the rhino species.

White rhinos are fast runners and can reach 50 km/h.

2 BLACK RHINO

SCIENTIFIC NAME:
Diceros bicornis
OTHER NAME:
Hook-lipped rhinoceros

COLOUR: Grey or brown skin

HORN: Two horns, with the larger one growing up to half a metre

COMMON SIZE: 3 metres in length, 1 tonne in weight

HABITAT: Savannah grasslands and forests of central and southern Africa

FOOD: Unlike white rhinos, black rhinos do not browse solely on grass. They eat leaves, plants and fruit as well as grass.

RED LIST EXTINCTION STATUS: Critically Endangered with only a few thousand left in the wild.

The black rhino is smaller than the white rhino. They are also more aggressive and will charge at each other, or any intruder in their territory.

Black rhinos use their pointed, upper lip like a finger to select plants to eat.

3 SUMATRAN RHINO

SCIENTIFIC NAME:
Dicerorhinus sumatrensis
OTHER NAME:
Hairy rhinoceros;
Asian two-horned rhinoceros

COLOUR: Dark brown hair

HORN: Two short horns, with the larger one growing to 20 centimetres long

COMMON SIZE: 3 metres in length, under 1 tonne in weight

HABITAT: Forests on the two Indonesian islands of Sumatra and Borneo

FOOD: Leaves, branches, twigs

RED LIST EXTINCTION STATUS: Critically endangered. May be fewer than 50 left alive in the wild.

SOUNDS

Sumatran rhinos make a variety of sounds to communicate with each other.

Their whistles and groans are so loud that the sound can carry over many kilometres through the forest.

The Sumatran rhino is the smallest rhino in the world.

BEHAVIOUR

Sumatran rhinos do not form herds and usually live alone.

Living in dense forests rather than flat savannahs means that Sumatran rhinos have evolved to be able to climb slopes that their larger relatives in other parts of the world do not need to do.

They can swim across rivers to get to food on the other side.

BODY

Unlike its larger African relatives, the Sumatran rhino has skin covered in short hair.

The upper lip is prehensile, meaning it can grasp and hold food.

There are thick skin folds around the body, but the skin is thinner than in the African rhinos.

4 JAVAN RHINO

SCIENTIFIC NAME:
Rhinoceros sondaicus

OTHER NAME:
Sunda rhinoceros; Lesser one-horned rhinoceros

COLOUR: Grey-brown hair

HORN: One 20 centimetres long horn that is rounded in shape

COMMON SIZE: 3 metres in length, 2 tonnes in weight

HABITAT: Lives only in a small rainforest area on the island of Java in Indonesia

FOOD: Using their upper lip, they select leaves, plants, fruit and twigs to eat.

RED LIST EXTINCTION STATUS: Critically endangered with only a few left in the wild.

The Javan rhino skin hangs in thick, hairless folds that look like armour.

POACHERS

The main reason for the decline of numbers of the Javan rhino is the action of poachers. Poachers kill Javan rhinos to take their horns to sell for their supposed medicinal properties.

SHARP TEETH

Unlike the African rhinos, Javan rhinos have sharp teeth at the front of the lower jaw. They use these to protect themselves if they are attacked by a predator.

Even though the horn is very small, poachers still kill Javan rhinos for their horns, to sell on the black market.

5 GREATER ONE-HORNED RHINO

SCIENTIFIC NAME:
Rhinoceros unicornis

OTHER NAME:
Indian rhinoceros

COLOUR: Grey skin without hair

HORN: One horn only that may grow to over half a metre long

COMMON SIZE: 3.5 metres in length, 2 tonnes in weight

HABITAT: Grasslands and bush forests of northern India and parts of Nepal, near sources of water

FOOD: Grass, leaves, plants, fruit and aquatic plants

RED LIST EXTINCTION STATUS: Vulnerable. There are about 4,000 living in the wild.

WATER

Greater one-horned rhinos spend a lot of their time in water, so they need to live near lakes, rivers and swamps.

Greater one-horned rhinos need to have access to water that is deep enough for them to wallow in to protect their skin from the sun.

SKIN

The skin is very thick and folded, with rounded bumps, which makes the greater one-horned rhino look as though it is wearing armour. Although this armour plating has no hair, some sparse hair grows around the ears and at the end of the tail.

FIGHTING

Males are known to fight over territory until one of them is so injured it will die from its wounds. The long horn is used as a weapon during these encounters. They also use their long, lower teeth to bite an opponent or a predator.

PREHISTORIC RHINOS

Modern rhinos are huge, but their prehistoric cousins were even bigger!

The *Paraceratherium* rhinos lived 30 million years ago. They were hornless, reached over seven metres long, and weighed an impressive 20 tonnes.

The *Elasmotherium* rhinos became extinct many thousands of years ago. They lived across parts of Europe and central Asia and probably had thick fur and a very long horn. Growing to over five metres long and weighing up to five tonnes, they were twice as big as a modern white rhino.

Coelodonta antiquitatis

The closest living relative of this woolly rhino from 2 million years ago is the Sumatran rhino.

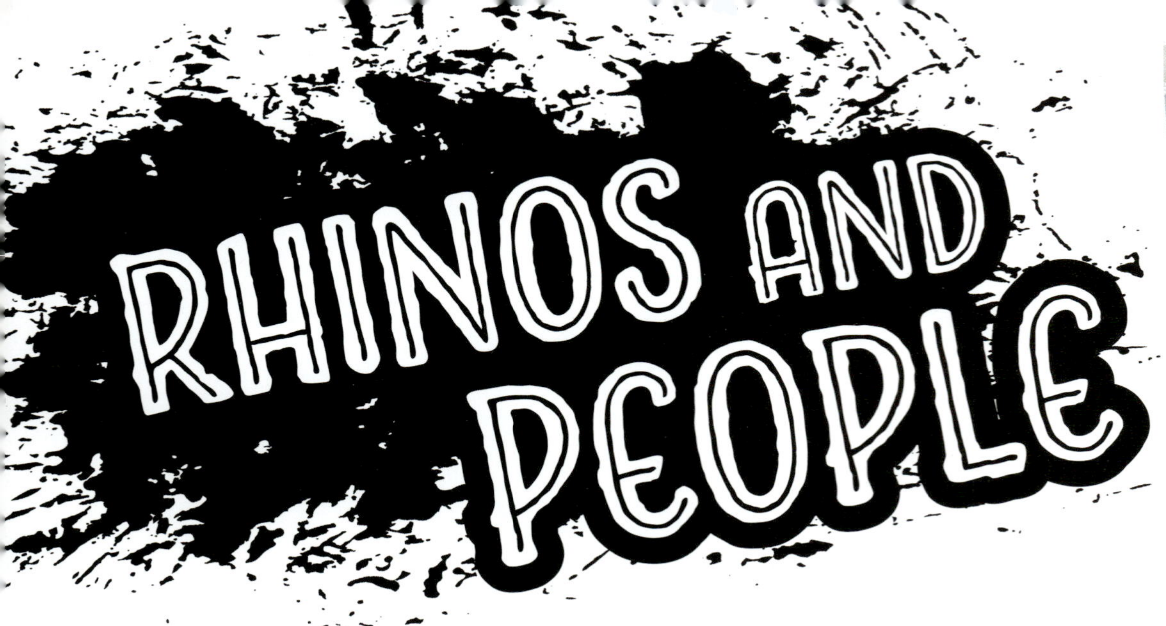

RHINOS AND PEOPLE

The main threats to the continued existence of rhinos are the activities of humans.

WAR

Many rhino habitats around the world have been affected by war. During conflict, protecting wildlife is not a priority, leaving rhinos especially vulnerable.

HABITAT

Increasing human population worldwide is responsible for the decrease in the natural habitat for rhinos.

BLACK MARKET

Many millions of people still believe that the rhino horn has legendary, medicinal properties. Because the horn is made of keratin, which is the same substance that forms hair, nails and hooves, this belief is clearly false. Despite this, poachers continue to kill rhinos to cut off their horns and sell them for very high prices on the black market.

BLACK MARKET

The black market refers to the illegal trade in animals and their body parts.

ZOOS AND RESERVES

Rhino horn is so valuable to poachers that, even in a zoo, rhinos are not safe. A white rhino was killed by poachers in 2017 when they broke into a zoo in France and took the animal's horn.

Some wildlife conservation managers have removed their rhinos' horns to keep the animals safe from being killed.

The two remaining northern white rhinos in the world are in a wildlife conservation area in Kenya, where they need to be guarded because of the threat from poachers.

The southern white rhino is the species that is most commonly seen in zoos around the world.

In zoos, rhinos need access to mud wallows to keep their skin healthy. Without its mud covering, a rhino's skin can crack and their body can overheat.

ENDANGERED RHINOS

RED LIST

The International Union for Conservation of Nature (IUCN) Red List is a catalogue of living things and their state of conservation. The Red List records all five living species of rhino and shows that they range in extinction threat from Near Threatened to Vulnerable and Critically Endangered.

Northern white rhinos are already almost extinct. The other living rhinos are not safe from poachers or from loss of their habitat, so they could face extinction in the future.

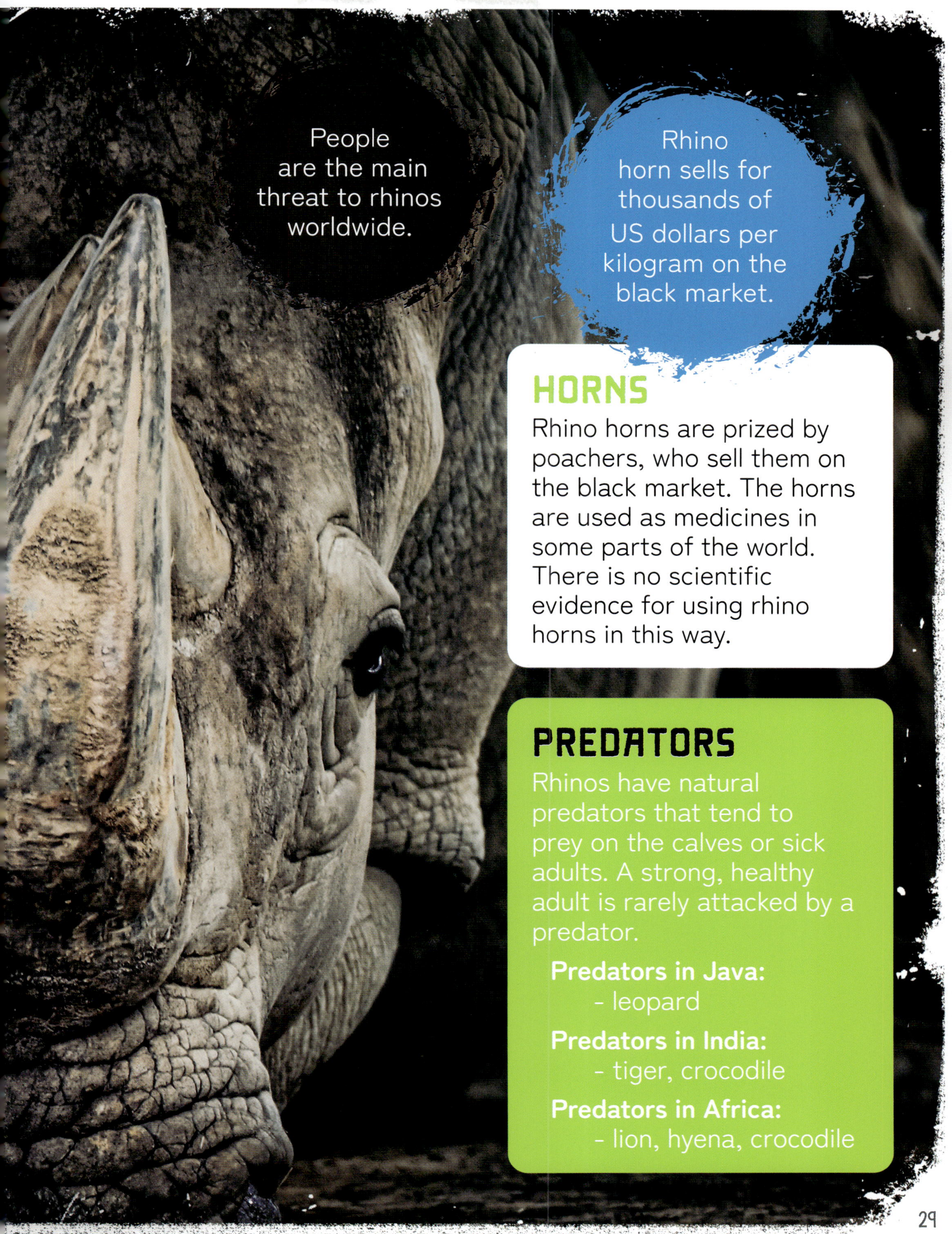

People are the main threat to rhinos worldwide.

Rhino horn sells for thousands of US dollars per kilogram on the black market.

HORNS

Rhino horns are prized by poachers, who sell them on the black market. The horns are used as medicines in some parts of the world. There is no scientific evidence for using rhino horns in this way.

PREDATORS

Rhinos have natural predators that tend to prey on the calves or sick adults. A strong, healthy adult is rarely attacked by a predator.

Predators in Java:
- leopard

Predators in India:
- tiger, crocodile

Predators in Africa:
- lion, hyena, crocodile

SORTING ANIMALS INTO GROUPS

Biologists divide all living things around the world into groups. They call this process classification.

ANIMALS ARE CLASSIFIED INTO TWO MAIN GROUPS:

VERTEBRATES

Vertebrates have a backbone

INVERTEBRATES

Invertebrates do not have a backbone

Vertebrates are further divided into five groups called classes:
MAMMALS (Mammalia)
BIRDS (Aves)
REPTILES (Reptilia)
AMPHIBIANS (Amphibia)
FISH
Humans are in the class called Mammalia. Rhinos are mammals and also belong in the class called Mammalia.

GLOSSARY

armour	strong outer covering to protect the body
black market	illegal trade in animals and their body parts
hefty	big and heavy
keratin	substance that forms hair, nails and hooves
megafauna	oversized animals that used to be common on Earth, but are now reduced to only a few species
poacher	person who kills or takes animals illegally from the wild
Red List	catalogue of living things and their state of conservation
savannah	grassland with few trees
solitary	alone
species	group of animals that is different from others

INDEX